The First 9 Discoveries

for a Rich Fulfilled Life Ahead

Hisae Sophia Dias

ISBN: 978-1-7644324-0-5
Printed in Australia

Published by
The Nine Discoveries Pty Ltd
theninediscoveries.com

Intellectual property notice:
The Nine Discoveries framework and the Creative Journey Formula™ system, including all related concepts, methodologies and materials, are the original intellectual property of Hisae Sophia Dias and are protected under copyright and trademark law. The commercial rights, licensing rights and distribution rights for this publication are held by The Nine Discoveries Pty Ltd.

Author: Hisae Sophia Dias

Disclaimer:
This book reflects the author's interpretations, insights, and perspectives. It is not intended as professional, legal, financial, or medical advice. All examples and scenarios are provided for illustration only.

National Library of Australia Cataloguing-in-Publication data:
A CIP record will be available from the National Library of Australia.

To my parents,
Atsuko Komine Dias and Tissa N.A.D. Dias

"The discoveries belong to no one.
They are as old as human hands reaching toward expression.
As ancient as the first mark made in sand.
As present as the child drawing beside you now."

THE FIRST 9 DISCOVERIES

FOR A RICH FULFILLED LIFE AHEAD

Hisae Sophia Dias

The Nine Discoveries Pty Ltd, Brisbane, Australia

Preface

The Grammar of Formation

There is a language older than words.

It speaks through the hand that reaches, the line that moves, the shape that closes.

It does not need to be taught. It needs only to be witnessed.

For over twenty years, I have sat with children as they discovered this language, not because I showed them how, but because something deeper was guiding them.

A baby's finger pressing into paint, leaving a single dot.
A toddler's hand dragging a crayon across paper, creating the first intentional line.
A three-year-old closing that line into a circle, eyes bright with recognition: I made a shape.

These are not accidents. They are discoveries.

And they follow a sequence so universal, so consistent across cultures and temperaments, that I began to wonder: What if this isn't just how children learn to draw? What if this is how consciousness learns to form itself?

A Pattern Recognized Across Time

I am not the first to notice that human development follows rhythms.

Jean Piaget observed that children move through stages of cognitive understanding, from sensing and moving, to imagining and symbolizing, to reasoning and reflecting.

Viktor Lowenfeld documented how artistic expression evolves, from scribbling to naming, from symbols to realism, from technique to personal voice.

Rudolf Steiner saw seven-year cycles in childhood, each marking a deepening relationship between self and world.

Howard Gardner identified the moment around age nine when children's vision races ahead of their hands, creating what he called "the crisis of literalism", the gap between what we imagine and what we can manifest.

Carl Jung understood that creation is not just making, it is individuation, the process by which the unconscious becomes conscious, the invisible takes form.

And Mihaly Csikszentmihalyi showed that creativity emerges not from chaos, but from flow, the delicate balance between challenge and skill, vision and patience.

Each of these thinkers, from different angles, saw the same truth: Human formation is not random. It follows patterns. It moves through stages. And creativity is not separate from this process, it is how the process reveals itself.

What I Have Observed

The Nine Discoveries I describe in this book emerged from direct observation, watching thousands of children over two decades discover the language of creativity.

I did not begin with theory. I began with presence, curiosity, and attention.

But as the pattern became clear, I realized I was seeing what others had seen before me: a universal grammar of formation.

The dot. The line. The shape. The colour. The flow. The trace. The rhythm. The integration. The form.

These are not techniques to master. They are stages of awareness to recognize.

They are the way consciousness learns to shape itself through contact with the world.

And they do not belong only to childhood.

The Nine Discoveries are not simply stages of art. They are the grammar of formation itself.

From this living grammar, I developed the Creative Journey Formula™, a structured system for teaching, applying, and transmitting these discoveries across classrooms, families, and institutions.

Why This Book, Why Now

We live in a time of acceleration.

Technology moves faster than integration. Information outpaces wisdom. Possibility exceeds our capacity to absorb what it offers.

Many of us feel like the nine-year-old whose heart races ahead of their hands, imagining futures we cannot yet embody, overwhelmed by the gap between vision and presence.

This book is an invitation to slow down.
To remember that formation cannot be rushed.
To notice the stages we pass through, not as obstacles, but as the path itself.

The Nine Discoveries offer a map for navigating a world that moves faster than formation allows. The Creative Journey Formula™ gives this map practical form, translating insight into lived structure. They remind us that creativity is not about speed. It is about depth.
That presence is not passivity. It is power.

That the patient work of bringing something into form, with our own hands, our own hearts, is an act of resistance, an act of becoming.

- - -

How to Read This Book

This is not a manual. It is a mirror.
Each chapter explores one discovery, not as a technique to master, but as a stage of awareness to recognize.

You may see your own children in these pages. You may see yourself.

You may remember moments when you made a dot, drew a line, filled a shape with colour.

And you may realize: I have been forming all along.

While every child's timing is unique, the sequence itself remains constant. Around age one, the dot appears. Around two, the line begins to move. By three, shapes form and boundaries emerge. At four, colour becomes identity. Five brings the flow of painting. Six discovers the magic of print-making. Seven reveals pattern and texture. Eight gathers fragments into collage. And by nine, construction brings everything into three-dimensional form.

These ages are guideposts, not rules. Some children move faster, others more slowly. But the order, from dot to construction, from single point to spatial form, follows the same rhythm across cultures and temperaments. This is not coincidence. It is how consciousness learns to form itself through contact with the world.

At the end of this book, you will find notes on the developmental thinkers whose work echoes what I have observed. Their insights ground this framework in decades of research. But the discoveries themselves belong to no one.

They are as old as human hands reaching toward expression.
As ancient as the first mark made in sand.
As present as the child drawing beside you now.

Welcome to the journey of formation.

It begins, always, with a single point.
A dot.

Introduction

A seed splits open in darkness.

A wave builds before it breaks.

A child's hand pauses before the first mark appears.

Every living thing carries a rhythm of becoming, and humans are no different. We are still forming.

For thousands of years, this process unfolded slowly, across generations, through seasons, in the quiet accumulation of lived experience.

But today, we live in an age where ten years of change arrives in ten months.

We celebrate acceleration as progress, yet we have often outrun our own depth. We begin to replace experience with information, presence with productivity, and imagination with automation.

And we start to see creativity as optional, when it has always been essential.

The pattern is the same everywhere: in a child drawing a line, in an adult navigating grief, in a community building trust, in a civilisation seeking to understand itself.

Formation begins in movement and continues in awareness.

It is not the work of childhood alone, it is the foundation of consciousness at every scale.

This book is an invitation to recognise that rhythm again, to see it not as something lost, but as something that has always been moving through us, waiting to be consciously lived.

You don't need to be an artist to enter this process.

You only need to be willing to notice, and to let what you notice change you.

Each chapter that follows explores one discovery, not as a technique to master, but as a stage of awareness to recognise.

You may read them in order, following the natural sequence, or return to whichever discovery calls you most strongly.

Some will see their own childhood reflected.

Others will notice where their awareness of formation faded, or where it still waits to be recognised.

This is not a manual.

It is a mirror.

And like all mirrors, it only works when you look directly into it.

Formation never stops.

It only waits to be noticed.

And it always begins the same way, with a single point of focus.

A dot.

Table of Contents

Closing Sections

Part I

Foundations of Form

Dot. Line. Shape.

Before anything can grow, it must begin.

But beginnings are quiet. They happen slowly, and mostly unseen.

In this part of the book, we explore the first three discoveries: the dot, the line, and the shape.

These are not just marks on paper. They are how all life begins to take form.

You'll notice that each one is simple. But do not mistake simplicity for smallness.

These are the discoveries that build your ability to focus, move with intention, and understand structure.

Every child begins here.
Every adult returns here.
And every system, whether natural or human-made, starts with these invisible foundations.

When we honour these early stages, we gain something rare in our time: clarity, calm, and the ability to see what truly matters.

Let us begin.

CHAPTER 1

The Dot
The Beginning of All Things

"In the beginning was the point. The first contact. The first decision to be."

You may not remember it, but you've already made a dot.

Not just with a pen or pencil, but with your focus. Your attention.

The moment you reached, or paused, or felt yourself connect with something, even for a second, you marked a beginning.

In early life, it happens before words, before explanation.

A baby's eyes follow light. A hand reaches out. A finger points.

There is no plan. No goal. Just presence and contact.

That's what the dot is: a moment of being fully here.

It's the start of every drawing, every idea, every relationship, every turning point.

And yet, in today's world, most people don't know where their dot is.

Their attention is pulled in every direction but never lands.

They feel ungrounded. Lost. Scattered.

The dot hasn't been made yet. They haven't paused long enough to say: "Here I am."

The dot is small, but it changes everything.
When you make it, you've crossed a threshold. You've gone from passive to present. From scattered to focused. From nothing to something.

And that's exactly where a rich and fulfilled life begins.
Not with big dreams. Not with knowing all the answers.

But with noticing what's right in front of you, and choosing to place your attention there.

- - -

In My Work with Children

I have seen this happen in the most subtle ways:

A fingertip pressing a dot of paint.
A finger dragging through spilled flour.
A quiet pause before marking a page.

No one tells them to do it.
It happens because the child is ready to become.
And the mark they make says: I'm here.

For Adults, the dot looks different.

It might be saying yes to something small.
It might be showing up to a quiet space.
It might be deciding that you will start again, even if you don't know how.

A rich and fulfilled life doesn't arrive all at once.

It begins in a single moment of contact, when you choose presence over distraction.

- - -

What the Dot Teaches

The dot reminds you that you are not behind.

You are not late.

You are already becoming, the moment you pause and notice.

You can begin again today. Right now. With one quiet point of focus.

In Adult Life:

The dot returns whenever we need to begin again.

When life becomes scattered, or when too many demands pull us in different directions, the dot reminds us to pause.

A single point of focus. One quiet place for attention.

Beginning again at any age starts with one simple dot.

Reflection Prompt:

What is your dot today?
What is the small, quiet place you're ready to give your attention to?

This is just the first step. In the next chapter, we'll explore how this first mark begins to move, how line brings direction, and how shape brings structure to your life.

CHAPTER 2

The Line

The First Language of Intention

"A line is a dot that went for a walk.", Paul Klee

The moment you make a line, something changes.

You're no longer just here, you're going.

You're moving, reaching, expanding beyond the single point.

A line is the first form of direction.

It is also your first language.

- - -

Even before we speak, we draw lines in the air, in sand, on windows, on our skin.

I remember watching my daughter when she turned one.
She received a gift, a small erasable drawing board with a stylus she had never used before.

There was no lesson. No instruction. Just her curiosity and her hands.

Within minutes, she was drawing spirals, loops upon loops.

Her eyes lit up. She was mesmerized.

And when she finished, she held the board up proudly, smiling, as if to say:
"Look what I did. Look what I can make."

There was no plan. Just discovery.

- - -

The Magic of the Line

That's the magic of the line, it reveals what's possible while you're doing it. It is intention without pressure.

Direction without needing to know the destination.

In the early stages of life, lines come naturally, sweeping across surfaces, flowing from the wrist, looping and stretching.

But later in life, lines are replaced by boxes, expectations, and checklists.

Freedom becomes structure. Movement becomes compliance. Creativity becomes correctness.

Returning to the Line

To live richly, we must return to the freedom of the line:

The wandering line.
The expressive line.
The questioning line.
The line that begins even when we don't know where it ends.

The Line and a Fulfilled Life

The line reminds us that movement matters.

Not all progress is visible.

Some of it happens in the space between the dot and the destination.

What begins as a playful gesture becomes, over time, the very act of showing up, again and again.

A child draws a line for fun.

An adult, in returning to that motion, creates a practice of presence.

There is joy in direction.

There is strength in momentum.

And there is healing in the freedom to wander.

In Adult Life:

The line returns whenever we need direction.

An adult who feels stuck, frozen, or unsure of their next step is simply waiting at the dot, still gathering presence, not yet ready to move.

The line is the moment we begin again.

It does not require certainty.

Only movement.

A line is a dot that trusted itself enough to go forward.

At any age, we can choose one simple direction.

One motion.

One small beginning.

The line is always waiting.

Try This:

Draw a line.

Start at one corner of the paper. Let it wander. Move it slowly or quickly.

Don't lift your hand.

When you're ready, finish at another edge of the page.

That's it. You've moved through space. You've left a trace.

The line brought movement. Now, what happens when that movement closes? When the line returns to meet itself? In the next chapter, we discover shape, and with it, the beginning of structure, boundary, and identity.

CHAPTER 3

The Shape
The Beginning of Understanding

"You do ill if you praise, and still worse if you reprove in a matter you do not understand.", Leonardo da Vinci

Shapes are everywhere, in nature, in everyday life, and in the way children begin to understand and communicate with the world.

Long before they can name them, children see shapes in trees, clouds, fruits, and shadows.

Nature becomes their first visual dictionary.

- - -

Learning to See

In the classroom, I often guide children through this way of seeing.

We once started drawing a cat by breaking down its body into simple shapes: the head as a circle, ears as triangles, the tail as a long curved line.

Then we moved on to something more familiar to Australian children, a koala.

I drew the same round head and asked them about the ears. At first, I added triangles.

They laughed and said, "That's not a koala!"

I asked, "Then what kind of shape are the ears?"

They told me, "Round!"

So I redrew the ears. Then I placed them low on the side of the head.

They giggled again, saying it looked like a monkey.

I asked, "So what do we do?"

They replied, "Put the ears higher!"

The drawing slowly evolved.

Then I asked, "What else makes it a koala?"

After a pause, one child said, "A koala has a big nose."

I asked, "What shape is it?"

They thought. "Not a triangle, not an oval... kind of like an avocado."

That moment showed how shape language is built, not from memorizing geometry, but from deeply observing life.

They recognized the difference between an oval, an egg, and an avocado shape, not by name, but by feeling and comparison.

This is how children learn to communicate: by rearranging shapes and adjusting placements.

What matters most is not correctness, but the flexibility and confidence to express.

- - -

The Boundary of "Mine"

Around this age, children become intensely protective of what they consider "mine."

If another child touches something they've claimed, they may protest strongly, not from selfishness, but from a developmental need to understand boundaries.

This is the same instinct that appears in their drawings: the line that closes becomes a shape.

The shape that defines becomes a space.

And the space they define on paper mirrors the space they're learning to claim in the world.

At age two, the child discovered movement through the line.

At three, they discover containment through the shape.

This is how identity begins, not as concept, but as lived experience of inside and outside, mine and not-mine, self and other.

Shape as Perception

Nature gives children all the shapes they need.

As adults, when we return to the lines we drew in Chapter 2, we can now notice how those lines became shapes, closed forms with meaning.

Shape, then, is not about perfection. It's about perception.

It teaches us how we see, how we compare, and how we express meaning by putting the right pieces together.

It's how we begin to make sense of what we see, and what we feel.

In Adult Life:

The shape returns whenever we need boundaries.

An adult who cannot say no, who feels stretched, or who loses themselves in others is simply revisiting the moment when the line closes and becomes a form.

Boundaries are not walls.

They are the edges that let us breathe.

At three, children discover mine.

At thirty, many adults rediscover it for the first time.

We meet shape again when we need to stand in our own outline,

to know where we end,

and to understand where connection begins.

The shape teaches us: you can be whole and still belong.

Try This:

Look at the lines you drew in Chapter 2.

Notice where any lines closed to form shapes, intentionally or accidentally.

Now, on a new page, draw three simple shapes: a circle, a triangle, a rectangle.

Observe them. Feel the difference between them.

One holds everything equally. One points. One stands.

Shapes carry meaning before we name them.

Shape gave us structure and boundary. But something is still missing. The shapes sit quiet, waiting. In the next phase, we discover what brings them to life, the language of colour, and with it, the beginning of emotion and identity.

Part II

The Language of Expression

The studio feels different on colour days.

There's a kind of hum in the air, quiet concentration mixed with curiosity. Brushes move, crayons scrape, water jars ripple softly on the tables.

When I ask the children to colour in with warm tones, something changes in their bodies.

They lean closer, press harder.

One child, colouring with a deep red, says suddenly, "It feels angry."

We weren't talking about emotions at all, but colour had found its way into feeling.

Later, when we paint the ocean, everything slows.

The room becomes quieter.

The children reach for blues and turquoise without being told.

They spread the colour gently, and the sound of the bristles softens. Someone whispers, "It feels calm."

The whole atmosphere shifts.

The same room, the same group of children, but a completely different vibration.

Warm colours bring energy, movement, and intensity.

Cool tones invite spaciousness, quiet, and release. Even the light seems to change.

That's when I realised: colour is not decoration.

It is language.

Before we name it, we feel it.

Before we describe it, we sense its temperature, its pulse, its rhythm.

It speaks directly to the body, bypassing logic, awakening something older and deeper than words.

When a child chooses red, yellow, or blue, they are not simply picking a crayon.

They are reaching for a frequency that matches what they feel or need.

In that moment, colour becomes expression, not of what they think, but of what they are becoming.

As adults, we still live by this hidden language.

We colour our homes, our clothes, our days.

We choose the tones that bring us back to balance.

We may forget to notice it, but colour continues to move through us, connecting the seen and the unseen, the mind and the emotion, the world and the self.

And that's when I understood:

Colour is the bridge between sensation and meaning.

It teaches us that emotion is not a reaction.

It is a vibration, a living dialogue between us and everything we perceive.

CHAPTER 4

The Language of Colour
Seeing with New Eyes

"Colour is a power which directly influences the soul.", *Wassily Kandinsky*

Around age four, a new kind of joy appears: the joy of colouring in.

Children at this age become deeply drawn to colouring books and printed outlines, not because they are told to stay inside the lines, but because the enclosed shapes offer a kind of invitation.

Colouring in is satisfying. It completes something. It gives life to a space.

But more precisely, it gives life to a shape.

- - -

The Power of Filling In

This instinct to fill in shapes is not about accuracy or neatness.

It is about presence.

When a child picks up a crayon and begins to colour in a shape, they are experiencing a kind of power: the ability to transform what's inside a boundary.

And this happens even before they truly begin to explore colour in the artistic sense.

Colour, at this stage, is about identity and completion.

That's why so many children at this age draw rainbows, again and again.

Rainbow cats. Rainbow skies. Rainbow houses.

When unsure what to draw, they colour rainbows.

These aren't realistic renderings. They are expressions of joy, awe, and wonder.

Colour becomes their way of saying "I am here."

- - -

The Magic of Primary Colours

At this stage, children are usually most interested in primary colours, red, blue, yellow, and basic secondary colours like green, orange, and purple.

Black and brown also appear, but not for contrast or tone.

They are not yet concerned with shadow or value.

What matters is saturation. Richness. Magic.

They do not need to be told the meaning of colour.

They can feel it.

Red feels different from blue. Yellow feels different from green.

The page becomes a place where emotion finds form, not through words, but through hue.

- - -

Colour as Language

As artist Helen Frankenthaler once said, "Every canvas is a journey you have to allow."

Colour is not a code to follow, it is an experience to enter.

And at this age, children enter it with their whole being.

When a child reaches for red, they are not just choosing a crayon.

They are reaching for energy, warmth, intensity.

When they choose blue, they are reaching for calm, space, quietness.

Colour becomes a language, a way to say something without words.

Before we name it, we feel it.

Before we describe it, we sense its temperature, its pulse, its rhythm.

It speaks directly to the body, bypassing logic, awakening something older and deeper than thought.

- - -

The Beginning of Expression

This is the moment when the child moves from structure (shape) to expression (colour).

At age three, they discovered boundaries.

At four, they discover what lives inside those boundaries, not just form, but feeling.

Colour doesn't just fill, it transforms.

It tells us where we are, how we feel, and what matters now.

This stage is not about teaching colour theory.

It is about watching colour become a language, a way to say something that has no other form.

And for the child, every stroke is an act of becoming.

In Adult Life:

Colour returns whenever we ask: Who am I?

An adult who feels grey, muted, unsure of what they stand for, they have lost contact with their own colour. They've been filling in shapes that others drew for them.

At four, children reach for the colour that matches what they feel. At forty, adults must sometimes remember how to do the same.

But here is what children know that adults often forget: you can choose a different colour tomorrow.

Identity is not fixed. It is not given once and held forever.

You can change. You can reach for a new hue. You can become someone you weren't yesterday.

What colour would you choose today? Not the one expected of you. Not the one you've always been. The one that feels like yours, right now.

Identity is chosen, one hue at a time. And it can be chosen again.

Activity for the Reader:

Return to the artwork you made after Chapter 2, the page of lines.

You may have noticed shapes emerging there.

Now, go further.

Choose one set of shapes you recognize and colour them in warm colours (red, yellow, orange).

Choose another set and colour them in cool colours (blue, green, purple).

You don't need to use every shape. Select the ones that feel connected.

Let your own sense of meaning guide the colouring.

Notice how the shapes come alive.

Colour doesn't just fill, it transforms.

It tells you where you are, how you feel, and what matters now.

Colour gave voice to what was silent. The shapes that once held only structure now hold emotion, identity, and presence. But colour, when still, is only potential. In the next chapter, we discover what happens when colour begins to move, when it flows, blends, and becomes painting.

CHAPTER 5

The Language of Painting
Letting Colour Flow

"Painting is just another way of keeping a diary.", *Pablo Picasso*

After finding boundaries in shape and filling them with colour, painting invites us to let those boundaries soften and blur, to explore, blend, and share space.

Paint is not just a material. It's a movement, a feeling, and a symbol of flow.

For a child, painting is a way to say something they don't yet have words for.

It is rhythm, release, and joy.

It's also sharing, of space, of materials, of discoveries.

And like a diary, it reflects the state of the painter in that moment.

The Magic of Mixing

At around five years old, children begin to show immense excitement with paint, especially when mixing colours.

Watching yellow and blue turn green, or red and white turn pink, becomes a magical experience.

They often don't want to stop.

The sensory joy of it all, seeing a colour change into their favorite, or something unexpected, is irresistible.

Mistakes don't exist in this phase. If one colour spills into another, they don't correct it, they celebrate it.

You'll often see several children sharing the same palette, experimenting without argument.

Harmony is key.

Painting shows children how to go beyond boundaries respectfully, creatively, and joyfully.

They start with a paintbrush, but soon they may want to use their hands.

This happens naturally, perhaps the brush slips, or they want to feel the magic of their favorite colour.

And because they're a little older, they now understand they shouldn't taste it (though that's not true for toddlers, who still require supervision).

The Beginning of Sharing

This willingness to share, to let your blue blend with someone else's yellow, is not just politeness.

It's the first conscious act of extending yourself beyond your own boundary.

At age three, the child discovered "mine."

At five, they discover something equally important: "ours."

The paint that flows from one palette to another is practicing what they'll spend a lifetime learning, how to remain yourself while connecting with others.

This is not merely social development. It is creative formation.

When a child shares paint, space, or discovery, they are learning that creativity can exist in relationship, not just in isolation.

They give, not because they are told to be kind, but because something inside has grown large enough to extend beyond the boundary of self.

- - -

The Dance Between Control and Freedom

Painting is the fifth Discovery because it teaches us the dance between control and freedom.

It allows us to soften the edges, to blend instead of define, to express instead of explain.

In life, this moment is about letting go of perfection and learning to respond to what appears.

As artist Helen Frankenthaler said, "There are no rules. That is how art is born, how breakthroughs happen. Go against the rules or ignore the rules. That is what invention is about."

Painting is the gesture of presence.

The moment you load a brush or finger with paint, you have committed to showing up.

Cy Twombly once described his process as "a kind of risk, like riding a bicycle fast downhill."

This is what children experience at the easel: speed, flow, surprise, and trust.

They are learning that expression doesn't need to be planned. It can emerge.

- - -

From Static to Moving Colour

In Chapter 4, colour was still, contained within shapes, held within boundaries.

Now, colour moves.

It flows across the page, mixes with other colours, leaves trails, creates gradients and surprises.
This is the beginning of creative flow, the state where the maker and the making become one.

At age four, colour gave identity.

At five, colour gives release.

It's best to provide only primary colours at this stage, red, yellow, and blue.

In Adult Life:

Painting returns whenever we need to soften our edges.

An adult who holds everything too tightly, who is afraid of mess, or who feels drained by constant control is simply meeting the discovery of painting again.

At five, children learn that colours move, and that something new is created when they meet.

Adults meet painting when life asks them to loosen their grip, to let emotions mix, to allow moments to flow without perfect order.

Painting teaches us that not everything needs a border. Some things become more beautiful when they blend.

We meet this discovery whenever life asks us

to be a little gentler with ourselves,

a little more open,

a little more willing to let things move.

Reflection Invitation:

Try this: Buy a small canvas or thick paper and just three primary colours.

Use a paintbrush at first, and then allow yourself to switch to your hands.

No rules. Just explore.

Feel the shift between tool and touch.

Notice how the colour moves, and how you do, too.

Use child-safe, non-toxic paint. Let your hands be part of the story.

This is your diary today.

From these three, a universe of colours can emerge, and children get to witness the surprise firsthand.

Painting brought movement and flow. Colour, once contained, now travels freely across the surface. But what happens when that moving image touches another surface? When it transfers, transforms, leaves a trace? In the next chapter, we discover printmaking, and with it, the art of surprise and the desire to be seen.

CHAPTER 6

The Printing
Art of Surprise

"I really love printmaking. It's like a mystery and you're trying to figure out how to rein it in.", Kiki Smith

Printmaking begins where painting leaves a trace.

A child presses a mark, and something appears, not exactly what they expected.

This is the moment when they discover: what you do on one surface can affect another.

It may be softer, blurrier, or even backwards.

This stage is not about perfection. It's about mystery, sharing, and letting go.

The moment of pressing the image is thrilling, like magic.

Children at this age begin experimenting with layering, repetition, and transfer.

Printmaking teaches them to observe, accept, and embrace surprise.

The Joy of Discovery

At around age six, children move from individual creation toward shared space.

They love group printing activities, where one child prints beside another, or on a shared surface.

They begin to value the process more than the outcome.

They rarely argue about mistakes. Instead, they laugh, repeat, and explore.

Using primary colours and simple materials, they experience the joy of unexpected results.

They discover how pressing a painted hand, carved potato, or textured object onto a surface creates something entirely new.

This is the age when they feel the need to be seen.

Leaving behind a print, on paper, clay, or soft material, feels like proof: "I was here."

- - -

The Desire to Be Noticed

Around age six, something shifts in a child's awareness.

They begin to seek recognition, not from vanity, but from a developmental need to know they matter beyond themselves.

Printmaking satisfies this perfectly.

The mark you leave becomes proof someone else can see.

The image you transfer says: "I was here, and it made a difference."

This is why children at this age love stickers, stamps, and handprints on clay.

Each one is both expression and evidence, a way of saying "I exist, and I want to be remembered."

At age five, the child learned to extend beyond their boundary through sharing.

At six, they learn to leave a visible trace, a mark that remains even after they've moved on.

This is not ego. It is the beginning of legacy.

- - -

Transfer and Transformation

Printmaking is the first symbolic experience of sharing and letting go.

You make something, transfer it, and it becomes something else.

It teaches children that their ideas can live beyond themselves, that expression isn't always controllable, and that beauty often lies in what's unplanned.

Recycled or overlooked objects, potato stamps, old lids, dried markers, gain value when used for print.

This reinforces care, transformation, and curiosity.

Even stickers, another way to transfer and leave a mark, are popular at this stage.

They show how much children enjoy creating visible evidence of presence.

The print is never quite what you imagined. It's softer, or bolder, or backwards.

And that's the lesson: what you release transforms.

- - -

The Mystery of the Reveal

There's a particular moment in printmaking that children love, the lifting.

The suspense of not knowing what will appear.

The peeling back of paper to reveal the image underneath.

In that moment, they learn something essential about creativity: you don't always control the outcome.

You press. You lift. You discover.

As Kiki Smith said, printmaking is "like a mystery and you're trying to figure out how to rein it in."

But the truth is, you don't always need to rein it in.

Sometimes the best discoveries come from what you didn't plan.

In Adult Life:

Printing returns whenever we need rhythm.

An adult who resists routine, feels trapped by repetition, or cannot hold steady habits is simply meeting Discovery Six again.

At six, children learn press, lift, repeat —

a simple rhythm that becomes trust.

Adults meet this rhythm when life asks them to build patterns that support them:

morning routines, steady work cycles, daily grounding.

If repetition feels heavy now, it is not failure.

It is an unfinished discovery.

The spiral always returns.

What felt restrictive at six can feel freeing at twenty-six or thirty-six.

Printing teaches us that rhythm is not confinement.

It is the pattern that helps life hold together.

Reflection Invitation:

Try this: Cut a potato in half, carve a shape or pattern into it, and use it as a stamp.

Try it on paper, clay, cardboard, or fabric.

Or press a painted hand onto paper and look at the reversed print.

Feel the texture. Notice how it changes.

Let it be imperfect. Let it be shared. Let it surprise you.

Printmaking taught us transfer and surprise. We learned that what we create can move beyond us, transformed. But now, something new begins to emerge, a desire for rhythm, repetition, and texture. In the next chapter, we discover pattern, and with it, the beginnings of design, order, and deeper awareness.

Part III

The Rhythm of Design

By now, the early foundation has been laid: the child has learned to make marks, form shapes, use colour, and express through paint and print. But around age 7, a new curiosity emerges - a desire for patterns, texture, combinations of collections, and finally structure.

It is no longer only about seeing—it's also about touching, sensing, comparing, balancing, and understanding. These discoveries unfold through repetition and variation-not as drills, but as natural rhythms of learning. Children begin to notice what happens when something repeats, when something breaks the pattern, and how small changes affect the whole.

The discoveries in this phase-Pattern, Texture, and Collage/Construction-invite the child to explore form not just as visual structure, but as a language of the world. Nature is filled with patterns. Relationships have texture. And the things we build carry our stories.

These are not just creative expressions. They are the beginnings of how humans organise experience and learn to live in a world of complexity. This phase is where rhythm, contrast, and cohesion begin to matter-laying the groundwork for future problem-solving, storytelling, and innovation.

CHAPTER 7

The Pattern and Texture
The Rhythm of Knowing

Before pattern becomes recognised, it is first experienced through print-ing. When children press paint-covered hands, stamps, leaves, or objects again and again, something essential begins: one mark becomes many. A single impression becomes a field. At first, they fill every space with repeated shapes, no rhythm, only joyful exploration. This is the earliest form of pattern. Printing teaches that repetition creates sequence, and when the paint dries, it leaves texture, raised, layered, and full of life. Even objects pressed into clay leave traces. Pattern and texture grow from this same root: the moment a child realises that one action, repeated, trans-forms the surface into something entirely new.

"Pattern is the language of nature.", Peter S. Stevens

By age seven, something shifts.

Children begin to search for rhythm, not just in sound, but in sight, space, and structure.

They are drawn to repetition, to making sense of what they see through order, sequences, and design.

Educational observers from Piaget to Montessori have noted this tran-sition: children who once resisted structure now seek it. What was once

external rule becomes internal rhythm. They notice patterns everywhere, in nature, in relationships, in the flow of daily life.
But it's not only pattern that calls them.

Texture becomes just as important.

They want to touch, press, compare, and explore the surface of things, rough, soft, bumpy, smooth.

They ask, without always saying it aloud: How does this feel? And why does it feel right?

- - -

Observing Pattern and Texture

In my ceramic classes, I see it unfold clearly.

Sticks scratched into clay. Imprints from shells. Fabric pressed into wet slabs.

Children create fish scales from fingerprints, spirals from bottle caps, wood grain from a toy car wheel.

They aren't just decorating. They're understanding.

This is a time of early design thinking.

Pattern and texture become tools for both logic and emotion.

Children begin to notice cause and effect: If I repeat this, it becomes something.

They test balance and symmetry without being taught the words. Unlike earlier phases where exploration was the goal, now they pause, observe, and often reflect on why something pleases them.

It is here they begin to compose.

- - -

The Language of Nature

Pattern speaks to nature's rhythm: waves, stripes on animals, leaves, music, seasons.

It offers safety, prediction, and a sense of belonging.

When a child notices that tree bark has lines, that flowers have symmetry, that days follow a rhythm, they are learning to read the world.

Texture, on the other hand, represents relationship.

It shows history, of material, of touch, of time.

While colour felt like personal identity, texture begins to resemble something wider, ancestry, family, even culture.

What's left on the surface is not just decoration, but memory.

The Desire for Order

Around this age, many children become fascinated with routines, schedules, and daily rhythms.

They want to know what comes next.

They notice when something is out of place, when someone behaves unexpectedly, when the usual sequence is disrupted.

This isn't rigidity. It's the beginning of design consciousness.

They are learning that order creates beauty. That repetition creates meaning. That rhythm creates safety.

Pattern is how we recognize home.

Texture is how we recognize love.

Both are languages older than words, languages we feel before we name.

- - -

Pattern and Texture in Creation

At this stage, children may:

- Create repeating patterns in drawing or painting
- Press textures into clay to see what emerges
- Arrange objects by similarity or difference
- Notice patterns in music, movement, or storytelling
- Return to the same creative process again and again, refining it

They are no longer content with pure spontaneity.

They want to see what happens when something repeats.

They want to feel the difference between surfaces.

They want to know: What makes this beautiful? What makes this true?

This is the moment when creativity becomes conscious craft.

When expression meets intention.

When the child becomes not just maker, but designer.

In Adult Life:

Pattern returns whenever we seek meaning in the noise of life.

An adult who feels lost, overwhelmed by details, or unsure how things fit together is simply revisiting the discovery of pattern.

At seven, children learn that repetition creates rhythm, that design creates beauty, that things can hold together.

Adults meet this discovery when life becomes complex and they begin searching for the thread that connects it.

Pattern is not control. It is recognition.

It is the moment we notice what repeats, in our choices, in our relationships, in the shape of our days.

Pattern teaches us how to read our lives and how our lives read us.

Reflection Invitation:

Spend a moment with a surface.

Clay, cardboard, stone, fabric.

Run your fingers across it. Feel the pattern, the rise and fall, the texture.

Now make your own.

Draw repeating lines. Press objects into clay or playdough.

Let children help you. Let yourself follow a rhythm.

Notice what patterns emerge, not just on the surface, but inside your mind.

Pattern and texture taught us to see the world's design, to feel its rhythms, its memories, its recurring beauty. But now, a new desire emerges. The child who has learned to notice and create patterns begins to gather, collect, and arrange. In the next chapter, we discover collage, and with it, the deep human need to belong while remaining whole.

CHAPTER 8

The Collage
The Story of Belonging

"Every child is an artist. The problem is how to remain an artist once we grow up.", Pablo Picasso

In this stage, children begin to collect, gather, and assemble.

They take scraps, broken toys, feathers, paper pieces, buttons, corks, and more, and suddenly see new meaning in them.

To an adult, it might look like junk.

But to the child, it's treasure.

And with those pieces, they start to build something entirely new.

This is the stage of collage.

Everything they've encountered so far, line, shape, colour, painting, print, pattern, and texture, can now be re-used, recombined, and re-imagined.

The discoveries are no longer separate. They are parts of a larger composition.

The Collecting Instinct

At this age, many children love collecting.

They gather similar things with subtle differences, sticks, bottle caps, stickers, feathers, fabric scraps, shiny wrappers.

And when asked to create something, they often return to their collections and find meaning in what they've kept.

This act of gathering reflects their growing sense of story.

A feather isn't just a feather, it might be part of a bird, or the wing of a dragon, or a crown for a royal figure.

A lid might become an eye, a wheel, or a button on a suit of armor.

I once collected feathers, white ones, grey ones, soft and stiff, small and wide.

Each day, I looked forward to finding a new one.

I didn't know why at first, but slowly I began to notice: each feather told me something different.

Some had fine wisps. Some curved. Some felt like they came from the same bird, just a different part.

I also collected bottle caps and seeds.

Over time, I realized, I wasn't just collecting. I was learning. Noticing. Connecting.

A collection holds stories. Even if you don't use them yet, they stay with you, waiting for their place in something larger.

Integration and Identity

A collage is not just random parts thrown together.

It's a reflection of memory, emotion, rhythm, and connection.

This is where a child's identity meets shared experience.

It's a desire to belong, while still contributing something unique.

In this stage, children may also begin to collaborate, sharing pieces, building side-by-side, or creating collective artworks.

Collaboration comes naturally when meaning is shared.

At age three, the child learned "mine."

At five, they learned "ours."

At eight, they learn "we", not as loss of self, but as belonging with self intact.

Collage teaches this beautifully: each piece remains distinct, yet contributes to something greater.

- - -

Cultural Echoes: Scrapbooking and Patchwork

Adults might recognize this process in the traditions of scrapbooking and patchwork quilting, forms that honor memory, gather fragments, and create meaning through careful arrangement.

What children do instinctively, cultures have formalized as cherished practices.

The quilt that tells a family's story, the scrapbook that holds a life's moments, these are collage in its deepest form.

Though many no longer scrapbook, it was once a treasured form of visual memory, collecting photos, mementos, magazine clippings, dried flowers, and notes to create a personal diary.

No formal instruction was needed. The act of keeping and arranging what mattered was enough.

Children do this naturally. And they do it with joy.

Some of the most beautiful things come from the pieces others leave behind.

- - -

Collage and Time

Collage also invites a new relationship to time.

When a child looks into a box of saved objects, they're remembering, imagining, and re-seeing.

It's not about being correct. It's about trusting their choices.

The surface of collage could be anything: cardboard, paper, canvas, wood.

And the act of arranging, moving pieces, trying different placements, seeing what feels right, is not just artistic. It's emotional intelligence.

They're learning to hold multiple truths at once.

That something broken can become part of something whole.

That different things can exist together without losing themselves.

That meaning emerges not from perfection, but from relationship.

- - -

From Flat to Form: The Bridge to Relief

As children continue working with collage, something begins to shift.

The materials they layer start rising off the surface, cardboard propped with glue, fabric bunched for texture, buttons creating shadow.

What began as flat arrangement evolves into relief, where depth emerges from layering.

This is the bridge between collage and construction, between gathering pieces and building form.

The child is now ready to move from surface to space, from the flat world of the page to the full dimensionality of sculpture.

In Adult Life:

Collage returns when life asks us to integrate.

An adult who feels divided or pulled in many directions is simply revisiting this discovery.

At eight, children learn that fragments can form a whole.

In adulthood, this becomes the work of gathering experiences, roles, and memories into coherence.

Nothing is wasted.

Every piece belongs somewhere.

Collage reminds us that we can assemble a life

from everything we have lived.

Reflection Invitation

What do you tend to collect or keep?

Look around your home, are there objects you've saved simply because they spoke to you?

Try making a collage with those items. Don't worry about it looking right. Let it feel right. And if you're working with children, invite them to show you their treasures.

Ask about what they've kept. You might be surprised by the stories they're ready to tell. You may discover that some of the most beautiful things come from the pieces others leave behind.

Collage taught us integration, how to gather fragments and create meaning, how to belong while remaining whole. But now, the pieces want to rise. What was flat begins to have depth. What was surface begins to have structure. In the final chapter, we discover construction, and with it, the fullness of form, the completion of the first spiral, and the shape of becoming.

CHAPTER 9

The Structure of Space
The Shape of Becoming

"Every act of creation is first an act of courage.", Pablo Picasso

By age nine, something changes again.

Children no longer want to simply paint, shape, or design, they want to build. They want to construct, balance, and form from every direction. They imagine not just surfaces, but spaces. Not just images, but systems.

This is the age of structure, when the world becomes three-dimensional in both imagination and intention.

Their hands reach forward eagerly, driven by a heart that now understands the pull of completion. They no longer only dream; they want to see their ideas stand. Clay becomes buildings, sticks become bridges, and paper becomes possibility.

But something else happens here, a tension between imagination and ability.

Their minds move faster than their hands can follow. Their inner world fills with visions: machines that move, creatures that make sound, sculptures that breathe smoke. They imagine motion, energy, life. But their fingers, still learning precision, cannot yet manifest what they see.

This is the first encounter with frustration.

Not the frustration of failure, but the frustration of becoming. Their vision has expanded beyond their current form, and their body must learn to keep up.

If guided well, this tension does not discourage. It refines. It teaches patience, perseverance, and the discipline of practice. It shows that mastery requires rhythm, that creation takes time, repetition, and the courage to stay with what is difficult.

This is the discovery of endurance.

- - -

The Bridge Between Vision and Skill

At this stage, children begin to see that creativity is not just emotion or play, it is construction. Every idea requires form, every dream demands skill. They learn that imagination without craft stays as fog, while craft without imagination becomes empty.

In their work, we begin to see both: the spark of vision and the struggle to translate it. Towers lean and collapse, but they rebuild. Sculptures crack, but they mend. They learn not just to make, but to stabilize.

This is the moment when creative energy begins to meet engineering instinct, the urge to test, balance, and make things work.

And yet, within this lies a deeper truth.

The Human Mirror

What we witness in the nine-year-old is not limited to childhood.

It is the same experience humanity now faces in the age of acceleration.

Our imagination, like theirs, has raced ahead of our capacity to build safely. Technology, artificial intelligence, and global systems move faster than our collective formation. We imagine futures that our emotional and social structures cannot yet sustain.

The result is the same tension: vision outpacing ability. And with it, the same frustration, the ache of wanting to see something realized before we are ready.

But this is not a crisis; it is a stage. A necessary part of growth. For both individuals and civilizations, frustration marks the boundary between what is imagined and what is possible.

- - -

Formation Through Construction

In the studio, a child building a tower learns more than balance.

They learn that gravity has rules, that materials resist, that shape depends on foundation. They learn that strength comes from patience, that form emerges through testing, and that beauty appears when the structure finally holds.

And so does life.

At nine, creation becomes a metaphor for being. To construct is to grow into oneself, to align intention with ability, and to endure the long process of making what the heart already sees.

This is how becoming takes shape.

Through the balance of patience and courage. Through the union of imagination and skill. Through the will to continue building, even when vision feels far away.

Because every structure, like every life, is built one steady layer at a time.

In Adult Life:

Construction returns when vision grows faster than ability.

An adult who feels the gap between what they imagine

and what they can yet build

is simply meeting this discovery again.

At nine, children dream in three dimensions

and struggle to make their hands keep up.

In adulthood, this becomes the work of patience —

developing skill, strength, and support

to match the size of the idea.

The gap is not failure.

It is formation.

Reflection Invitation:

Take a moment to build something, anything.

Stack stones, arrange books, shape clay, or construct a small form from what surrounds you.

Feel how your hands move, how your mind plans, how your patience responds when it doesn't stand at first. Notice the rhythm between thinking and doing, the slow harmony of creation.

Now step back and look. See not just the structure, but yourself within it.

This is the shape of becoming, the meeting point between imagination and form, vision and patience, dream and endurance.

And like every discovery before it, it reminds us:

Formation never ends. It only deepens.

What Comes Next

The first spiral is complete.

From dot to construction, from single point to spatial form, we have traced the journey consciousness takes as it learns to shape itself through creativity.

But formation does not end at age nine. It continues, spiraling through adolescence, adulthood, and into the collective patterns of culture itself.

The discoveries you've read about in this book reappear throughout life, each time asking us to return to presence, to notice where we are, to honor the stage we're in rather than rushing past it.

In the companion work to this book, The Last Acceleration, I explore what happens when culture moves faster than formation allows, when technology, information, and possibility outpace our capacity to integrate what they offer.

The nine-year-old whose heart races ahead of their hands is practicing what humanity practices collectively: learning to hold the gap between vision and embodiment with patience, courage, and trust.

If this book has helped you recognize your own formation, or your child's, I hope you'll continue the journey with me.

Through the Creative Journey Formula, including future programs and digital tools, this work continues to evolve in lived practice.

Formation never ends. It only deepens.

And the next spiral has already begun.

THE JOURNEY AHEAD

Formation does not end with childhood.
The Nine Discoveries continue to unfold throughout life,
returning every decade in a deeper spiral.

The discoveries we met at one, two, or six
return again at sixteen, twenty-six, and thirty-six—
shaped by new experiences,
new relationships,
and new capacities of understanding.

When a discovery was interrupted in childhood,
life brings it back.
Not as a correction,
but as an invitation to complete what was paused.
Nothing is lost.
The spiral is patient.

We meet the dot again when we begin anew.
We meet the line when direction is needed.
We meet shape when boundaries must be felt.
We meet colour when identity shifts.
We meet rhythm when life asks for stability.
We meet pattern when we search for meaning.
We meet collage when the pieces need to come together.
We meet construction when our vision grows larger than our hands.

The Nine Discoveries are not stages we leave behind.
They are companions that return
at every turning point,
every transition,
every new beginning.

This book has given you the first layer of formation.
The next layers await—
deeper, wider, and shaped by the life you are living now.

The journey continues,
and it always begins again
with one quiet dot.

APPENDIX

Developmental Foundations
of The Nine Discoveries

The sequence described in this book, from dot to line, shape to colour, painting to printmaking, pattern to construction, emerged from twenty years of observing children discover the language of creativity.

Only after the pattern became clear did I explore what other observers had documented. I was surprised, and humbled, to discover that developmental theorists, educators, and philosophers had noticed similar patterns, though through different lenses.

Here is a brief overview of how The Nine Discoveries align with established frameworks of human development:

Jean Piaget (1896–1980)

Swiss psychologist; pioneer of cognitive development theory

Piaget identified stages through which children's thinking evolves: from sensorimotor (learning through physical interaction) to preoperational (symbolic thinking) to concrete operational (logical reasoning). The Nine Discoveries follow this same progression, beginning with the dot (sensorimotor presence) and moving toward construction (concrete operational planning and spatial reasoning).

Relevance: Shows that creative formation mirrors cognitive development; both follow universal, stage-based sequences.

Viktor Lowenfeld (1903–1960)

Austrian-American art educator; author of Creative and Mental Growth

Lowenfeld documented how children's artistic expression evolves through predictable stages: scribbling, naming, schematic representation, dawning realism, and pseudo-naturalistic expression. He observed that around age nine, children experience frustration when their vision exceeds their technical ability, the same gap documented in Chapter 9 of this book.

Relevance: Validates that the Nine Discoveries are not invented but observed patterns in how artistic consciousness naturally unfolds.

Rudolf Steiner (1861–1925)

Austrian philosopher; founder of Waldorf education

Steiner identified seven-year cycles in child development, with age seven marking a major transition from imaginative to reasoning consciousness. His educational approach emphasizes rhythm, pattern, and sensory experience, all central to Phase 3 of The Nine Discoveries (ages 7–9).

Relevance: Affirms that formation follows natural rhythms; children seek structure and pattern at predictable developmental moments.

Howard Gardner (1943–present)

American psychologist; creator of Multiple Intelligences theory

Gardner's research on artistic development identified what he called the "crisis of literalism" around ages 9–10, when children become acutely aware of the gap between what they imagine and what they can produce.

Relevance: Explains why construction (age 9) is both culmination and crisis; the vision-execution gap is not failure but necessary developmental tension.

Carl Jung (1875–1961)

Swiss psychiatrist; founder of analytical psychology

Jung understood creative expression as individuation, the process through which unconscious content becomes conscious, formless potential takes shape, and the self discovers wholeness.

Relevance: Positions the Nine Discoveries as more than artistic technique; they are stages of consciousness becoming visible to itself through form.

Mihaly Csikszentmihalyi (1934–2021)

Hungarian-American psychologist; researcher of flow and creativity

Csikszentmihalyi's flow theory describes creativity as emerging from the balance between challenge and skill. Around age nine, many children feel this imbalance acutely, their imaginative challenge outpaces their technical skill. Those who learn to tolerate this gap develop creative resilience.

Relevance: Validates the frustration documented in Chapter 9 as natural developmental phenomenon; formation requires patience at the edge of capacity.

Convergence of Insight

These thinkers approached human development from different traditions, psychology, education, philosophy, spirituality, yet all recognized the same truth:

Formation follows patterns. Growth moves through stages. And creativity is not separate from development, it is how development reveals itself.

The Nine Discoveries offer a creative lens on what these observers documented from other angles. Where Piaget saw cognitive stages, where Steiner saw rhythmic cycles, where Jung saw archetypal unfolding, this book sees the visible trace of consciousness learning to form itself through making.

The Creative Journey Formula carries this understanding into structured educational practice.

The discoveries belong to no single tradition. They are as old as human hands reaching toward expression, as present as the child drawing beside you now.

Dedication and Authorship Reflection

This work is not mine alone. It was formed through a life shaped by many hands, many hearts.

From my earliest years, I was drawn to babies and children, not just to teach, but to observe, to feel, to follow. That attention was nurtured beside my grandfather, a spiritual teacher of quiet strength. I lived with him, travelled with him, and absorbed the rhythm of a life lived with presence and meaning.

My father, a philosopher and scientist, opened the door to thought. His voice shaped my own questions and gave me the freedom to ask without end.

My mother, grounded and radiant, taught me not to carry life too seriously, but to live it fully, with resilience and laughter. Quietly, she is also a gifted artist. A master of kimono-making, skilled in Japanese Flower arrangement (Ikebana), and even painting, she creates purely for the joy of it.

My sister has walked beside me always, in childhood and now, supporting the woman I have become. Her strong sense of aesthetics, expressed through fashion and beauty, deepened my own love for art and its place in daily life.

To my husband, who has stood with me through the shaping of a family, through moments both soft and difficult, thank you for giving me space to grow stronger.

And to my three children: raising you has been a gift, but learning from you has been even greater. Your presence, your stories, your drawings, your discoveries, you are in every word of this book. Without you, none of it would have taken form.

And not to forget Rocky, our family dog, my companion, my quiet teacher. You made me tougher, healthier, and more grounded. Without you, I wouldn't have walked through the forest each morning, where imagination stirred and discoveries found their way to me.

Thank you.

To the friends who believed in me, who stretched me, who encouraged me to begin, thank you for seeing the path before I could. Your support has been one of my greatest gifts.

To the parents who trusted me with their children, thank you for your presence, your patience, your encouragement.

And to the children I've taught, you have been my greatest teachers. You've shown me how imagination moves, how creation speaks. I have likely learned more from you than I've ever taught. No matter your age or where life takes you, I hope you carry these creative sparks with you. I hope you keep using your hands, your eyes, your imagination, and that all you've discovered continues to help you, Flourish.

To my grandmother, whom I knew only as a child, but whose calm trust and quiet support of our family left a lasting impression. Your presence taught me many things in ways only a grandmother can.

To my cousins, especially those in other countries, who supported me through online connections and constant care. You have been like siblings, helping me feel seen and strong across distances.

To my extended family and community, thank you for listening, including me, and making me feel that I belong. Your support has been deeply felt.

To my cousin who recently passed, your love for knitting and the meditative strength you found in your art left a lasting imprint. I hold you in this book with quiet reverence.

And to my future students, parents, guardians, and all those in the wider community I've yet to meet thank you in advance. You are already part of this story. Your books, your voices, your kindness have helped shape my path. I hope one day we can meet in person.

To the great thinkers, spiritual teachers, and voices, past and present, who have guided my inner world, thank you.

About the Author

Hisae Sophia Dias was born in Tokyo and now lives in Brisbane, Australia. She was educated at the International School of the Sacred Heart, where she moved naturally between cultures, languages, and ways of seeing.

She later studied at The Art Institute of Boston on a full scholarship, beginning her work as a graphic designer. Her career has spanned advertising, publishing, packaging, and branding, but through it all, she followed a deeper calling, to understand how creativity shapes us as human beings.

Sophia has taught both adults and children for over two decades, and founded an art education practice in Brisbane that has welcomed thousands of students. Her work bridges art, education, and human development, helping people rediscover imagination as a lifelong source of clarity and joy.

She is the creator of The Nine Discoveries framework and the Creative Journey Formula educational system.

This book is the first in a series tracing the patterns of formation, from childhood through adulthood, and into the collective evolution of human consciousness.

The final discovery is not an ending, but a turning

What was once shape becomes space. What was once structure becomes possibility.
Every mark, colour, and form has brought us to this moment, the threshold between
what is made and what is still becoming.
The Nine Discoveries are not a ladder to climb, but a rhythm to return to.
They spiral through life, appearing again each time we grow into a new understand-
ing of ourselves and the world.
Formation never ends. It only deepens. And from here, the next spiral begins.

A journey into the earliest language of human creativity,
from the first mark to the full expression of imagination.

The First 9 Discoveries reveals how humans form meaning
long before words, long before knowledge,
through the simple acts of seeing, touching, noticing, and creating.

This first edition is offered with gratitude to the families
and communities who walked this journey with me.

Hisae Sophia Dias

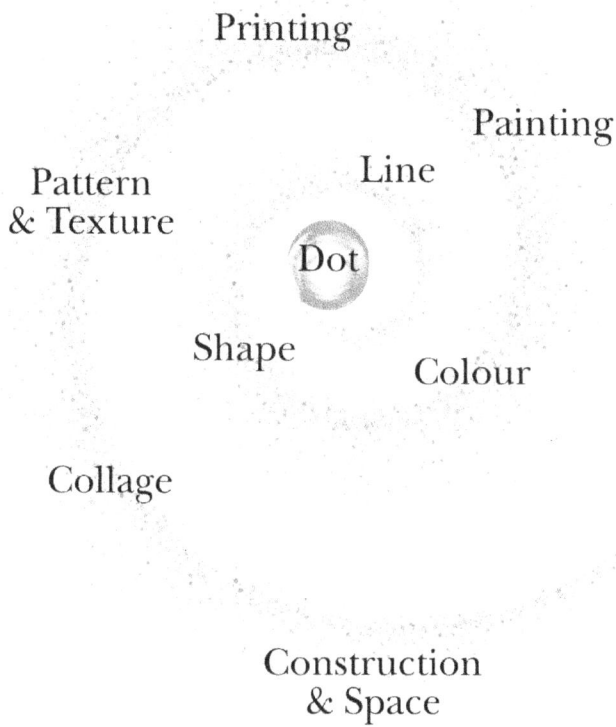

Printing

Painting

Line

Pattern
& Texture

Dot

Shape

Colour

Collage

Construction
& Space

www.ingramcontent.com/pod-product-compliance
Lightning Source LLC
Chambersburg PA
CBHW051247020426
42333CB00025B/3097